MW01249238

JUMPSTART YOUR DAY WITH THE LORD #1

Thirty Day Readings

MOSES LEE RADFORD

Dedication

I am indebted to my family: Calvonia my wife for always encouraging me to put my writings in print; my children Mario, Casondra, and Christian for sharing their father with the Lord and churches; and so many others, especially other children.

I am indebted to the churches that I have served: New Mount Zion Missionary Baptist Church of Depoy, Moore's Chapel Missionary Baptist Church of Nortonville, and First Missionary Baptist Church of

Greenville, all in Kentucky. They helped me in my early years in the ministry.

I am especially indebted to First Baptist Church of Nicholasville, Kentucky for they have encouraged me in countless ways in these twenty-four years of serving them. Much of what I am today is because the Lord has allowed me to serve a great church.

Also I am indebted to Pleasant Hill Missionary Baptist Church of Christian County, Kentucky. This is where I was born again, learned of the Lord, learned to teach the Word, was licensed to preach the Gospel of Christ, ordained as a Baptist minister, and then sent out to serve as a pastor.

Most of all, I am indebted to my Lord and Savior Jesus Christ for placing me in the ministry and blessing me with a heart and mind to study His Word to preach and teach others to His glory and honor.

In Memory

*T*his book is in memory of my parents, Edward Radford and Mary Jessup Radford. My mother said she named me "Moses" because she knew that I would be a leader. My father saw something in me when I was a teenager that caused him to say that the Lord had given me wisdom. I am thankful for everything they did to make me what I am. The Lord used them to make me.

My father was a preacher/pastor and my mother was a teacher/missionary. I wish I had written this before they went home to be with the Lord. However, I thank them for their love and influence.

Table Of Contents

Introduction

*T*his book consists of thirty short readings that will encourage you as you spend some time in the Word with the Lord. You may choose to read one reading daily in a month to get your day started with the Lord, or you may choose to read in the evening. Do whatever works best for you. It is my desire that this book will be a blessing to you. There are many subjects covered ranging from hearing the voice of the Lord to caring for the poor. As you read them, you will see what the Lord has to say about matters of life that will bless you, and He wants you to be a blessing to others.

This is one of a few devotional books that are coming out soon if the Lord permits. These books may scrve a great purpose in your life in days to come; one never knows. There may be a dark moment, and the Lord can bring to your mind something that you have read in one of the devotional books. You will be able to get it and read it again, and then your spirit is lifted. If this happens, please give God the glory, praise, and honor.

Chapter 1
Making Known the Lord's Words

Exodus 4:27–31 (KJV)

And the LORD said to Aaron, Go into the wilderness to meet Moses. And he went, and met him in the mount of God, and kissed him.

And Moses told Aaron all the words of the LORD who had sent him, and all the signs which he had commanded him.

And Moses and Aaron went and gathered together all the elders of the children of Israel: And Aaron spake all the words which the LORD had spoken unto Moses, and did the signs in the sight of the people.

And the people believed: and when they heard that the LORD had visited the children of Israel, and that he had looked upon their affliction, then they bowed their heads and worshipped.

*G*od had called Moses to go into Egypt to get His people out and to bring them to the Promised Land. Moses had said to the Lord that he could not speak plain but the Lord had a plan to help him. The Lord brought Moses and Aaron together. He was happy to see his brother for he had not seen him in a long time.

When the Lord brings family together they ought to be glad and pleased. Moses told Aaron what the Lord had said to him and about the signs of the Lord.

God used Aaron to speak unto the Children of Israel for Moses had a speech problem. Since Moses had such a problem with speaking, the Lord fixed it by giving him Aaron. Aaron had no problem in understanding his brother. When there is a problem in life the real answer is in the Lord and His Word. The Children of Israel had a listening ear to hear the Word of the Lord through Aaron as Moses gave it to him. The children of Israel worshipped the Lord because they believed what they were told about the God of glory. The Word is given to believers and it should lead to obedience and worship of the Lord.

Chapter 2
Take in God's Word

Psalm 119:9–16 (KJV)

Wherewithal shall a young man cleanse his way?
by taking heed *thereto* according to thy word.
With my whole heart have I sought thee: O let
me not wander from thy commandments.
Thy word have I hid in mine heart, that I might
not sin against thee.

Blessed *art* thou, O LORD: teach me thy
statutes.

With my lips have I declared all the judgments
of thy mouth.

I have rejoiced in the way of thy testimonies, as
much as in all riches.

I will meditate in thy precepts, and have respect
unto thy ways.

I will delight myself in thy statutes: I will not
forget thy word.

*T*he Word of the Lord ought to mean more
to believers than anybody else's word. The
Lord's Word is to be read, learned, believed, and lived.
As one reads this passage of scripture, he will see the
answer to the question that is asked, "Wherewithal shall

a young man cleanse his way?" There are some things that a believer must do if he wants to be cleansed. He cannot be cleansed through stuff of this world; all the world has to offer will cause man to be dirtier than ever. Therefore, get in the Word of the Lord so you can be cleansed and presentable to Him.

1. Give your attention to the Word for it has something to say to you.

2. Seek the Word with your whole heart; it will keep you from being lost.

3. Hide the Word in your heart for doing so will cause you to think.

4. Position yourself so the Lord can teach you His Word.

5. Speak the Word of the Lord for there is power in it.

6. Rejoice in how the Lord has used His Word to deliver you.

7. Allow the Word to be the center of your thoughts as you go through the day.

8. Delight in the Word, and you will have something to hold on to.

As you take in these thoughts, you will find that the Lord will give you the strength needed for the trips of life. Anything that one cares about, he will treasure by holding it dear to his heart. The Word of the Lord ought to be the greatest treasure to hold on to dearly.

Chapter 3
Do What the Lord's Word Says

Jeremiah 35:12–17 (KJV)

Then came the word of the LORD unto Jeremiah, saying,

Thus saith the LORD of hosts, the God of Israel; Go and tell the men of Judah and the inhabitants of Jerusalem, Will ye not receive instruction to hearken to my words? saith the LORD.

The words of Jonadab the son of Rechab, that he commanded his sons not to drink wine, are performed; for unto this day they drink none, but obey their father's commandment: notwithstanding I have spoken unto you, rising early and speaking; but ye hearkened not unto me.

I have sent also unto you all my servants the prophets, rising up early and sending *them,* saying, Return ye now every man from his evil way, and amend your doings, and go not after other gods to serve them, and ye shall dwell in the land which I have given to you and to your fathers: but ye have not inclined your ear, nor hearkened unto me.

Because the sons of Jonadab the son of Rechab have performed the commandment of their father, which he commanded them; but this people hath not hearkened unto me:

Therefore thus saith the LORD God of hosts, the God of Israel; Behold, I will bring upon Judah and upon all the inhabitants of Jerusalem all the evil that I have pronounced against them: because I have spoken unto them, but they have not heard; and I have called unto them, but they have not answered.

*T*he Lord expects His Word to be heard and obeyed. He had the prophet Jeremiah tell the people of Judah that they had not been listening to Him; therefore they were not living up to His Word. The Lord draws their attention to an earthly father whose sons were living in obedience unto Him in all things.

Jeremiah points out that Judah had not obeyed the Lord's commands. They had turned down the prophets that the Lord had sent to give them messages and, in doing so, they were turning down the God of glory. They were in line for a punishment from the Lord for their disobedience. Now if you read the next two verses, you will discover how blessed the sons of Jonadab were for being obedient.

There are blessings in store for the people of God when they obey Him for He rewards obedience. Believers are expected to live in obedience to the Lord each and every day, not just on Sundays. The Scripture teaches that saints are to live a holy life for they have been changed by the power of God through Christ Jesus, and by the aid of the Holy Spirit. It is not enough for people to call Jesus "Lord" and live in disobedience, for there is no proof that they belong to Jesus. God is the Father of those who have accepted Jesus Christ as Lord and Savior. Because He is Father, it is no more than right to obey His Word.

Chapter 4
Live in the Love of Jesus
John 15:1–15 (KJV)

I am the true vine, and my Father is the husbandman.

Every branch in me that beareth not fruit he taketh away: and every *branch* that beareth fruit, he purgeth it, that it may bring forth more fruit.

Now ye are clean through the word which I have spoken unto you.

Abide in me, and I in you. As the branch cannot bear fruit of itself, except it abide in the vine; no more can ye, except ye abide in me.

I am the vine, ye *are* the branches: He that abideth in me, and I in him, the same bringeth forth much fruit: for without me ye can do nothing.

If a man abide not in me, he is cast forth as a branch, and is withered; and men gather them, and cast *them* into the fire, and they are burned. If ye abide in me, and my words abide in you, ye shall ask what ye will, and it shall be done unto you.

Herein is my Father glorified, that ye bear much fruit; so shall ye be my disciples.

As the Father hath loved me, so have I loved you: continue ye in my love.

28

If ye keep my commandments, ye shall abide in my love; even as I have kept my Father's commandments, and abide in his love.

These things have I spoken unto you, that my joy might remain in you, and *that* your joy might be full.

This is my commandment, That ye love one another, as I have loved you.

Greater love hath no man than this, that a man lay down his life for his friends.

Ye are my friends, if ye do whatsoever I command you.

Henceforth I call you not servants; for the servant knoweth not what his lord doeth: but I have called you friends; for all things that I have heard of my Father I have made known unto you.

*I*t is the responsibility of each believer to abide in the Lord. The connection between the vine and branches is to give a picture of how Christ and believers are connected. There is no way for branches to bear fruit if they are not connected to the vine. They will lie down on the ground and dry up and die. This is what happens to a believer when he takes himself away from the Lord and His church. A believer cannot grow and produce fruits apart from the Lord and His church. It is very important for saints to abide in Christ for as the branch gets its strength from the vine so it is with the saints; they get their strength from the True Vine.

Christ is the True Vine, and believers are to abide in Him each and every day.

If saints are going to bear fruit, they must abide in the love of Christ. The only way the world can tell that believers are in Christ is by how they love each other. Therefore saints are to stay in the love of Christ, so it will be expressed in and through their lives. Jesus points out in this passage that believers are loved as He is loved by His Father, and they are to keep loving in that same manner. The branches are to live in obedience to the Vine; in keeping His commandments this is evidence of abiding in His love. The end result of abiding in the love of Christ will be reaching others for Him and causing them to abide in the same love.

Chapter 5
Life without an End

John 17:1–5 (KJV)

These words spake Jesus, and lifted up his eyes to heaven, and said, Father, the hour is come; glorify thy Son, that thy Son also may glorify thee:

As thou hast given him power over all flesh, that he should give eternal life to as many as thou hast given him.

And this is life eternal, that they might know thee the only true God, and Jesus Christ, whom thou hast sent.

I have glorified thee on the earth: I have finished the work which thou gavest me to do.

And now, O Father, glorify thou me with thine own self with the glory which I had with thee before the world was.

This is one of the most outstanding prayers in the Holy Bible, though there are many prayers by different people. This prayer was prayed by our Lord and Savior Jesus Christ as He was on His way to the cross to give His life for fallen humanity. This prayer is the Lord's Prayer but not the one that is traditionally called the Lord's Prayer in Matthew 6. That prayer is the Model Prayer that Christ gave the disciples as an example. In the prayer of John 17, Christ is praying an intercessory prayer. An intercessory prayer is praying on the behalf of others. This is what Christ was doing as He lifted up His eyes to heaven. Please take note that Jesus Christ gave recognition to His Father as He prayed. Believers are to follow the Lord when they pray; they should always recognize the Heavenly Father.

Jesus Christ completed the mission that the Father sent Him to do; that is to give eternal life. He made known through His preaching and teaching that eternal life is available to all who would hear. The Father placed ones in the hands of His Son, and He gave eternal life to all of them except Judas for he was the son of perdition (John 17:12). What is eternal life? It is life without an end and life with quality. There is no better life than the life that the Lord gives. The life He gives is eternal life, and this life is an everlasting life to those who accept Jesus Christ. The eternal life begins the moment a sinner accepts Jesus Christ as Savior. It causes him to live a life, looking forward to living with Christ Jesus forever. He has promised life with Him forever and experiencing this life leads one to know that the Father is the only true and living God. All saints ought to be thankful that they have something that they cannot ever lose because this life is eternal, and one cannot be taken out of the Father's hand (John 10:28–29).

Chapter 6
Grace Came with Jesus

Titus 2:11–15 (KJV)

For the grace of God that bringeth salvation
hath appeared to all men,

Teaching us that, denying ungodliness and
worldly lusts, we should live soberly, righteously, and godly, in this present world;

Looking for that blessed hope, and the glorious
appearing of the great God and our Saviour
Jesus Christ;

Who gave himself for us, that he might redeem
us from all iniquity, and purify unto himself a
peculiar people, zealous of good works.

These things speak, and exhort, and rebuke with
all authority. Let no man despise thee.

*M*an was in a condition for which he needed
divine help. The help that he needed had to
come from the Father. He sent His Son Jesus Christ to
bring the grace that man needed, and with the grace,
came salvation. The salvation of the Lord is for all mankind. There is no one so sinful that the grace of God
cannot reach them. The worst of all men can receive

the grace of God through Jesus Christ and have salvation forever. John points out that grace and truth came by Jesus (John 1:17). Believers are taught by this grace what to deny and accept and how to live while here in this world. Saints are to conduct themselves in a manner that the world will not blame them for not seeing Jesus in them. The grace of God helps saints to live in the right manner so others can see the Lord.

Believers are to look forward to something great; it is true that the best is yet to come. It is coming with the Lord Jesus Christ at His second coming. He is coming back someday to take away all those who have been saved by His grace. Jesus Christ paid the price to redeem fallen man from his sins, and He has cleansed him from all unrighteousness. Since God's grace has come, all need to know that the Lord has a purpose for them. This is why He has made them a special people. The Lord expects believers to bear fruit and more fruit and much fruit (John 15) for fruit will be expressions of the grace of God in the lives of His people. One can easily remember that grace is a gift that he does not deserve. Another way to remember it is to look at the acronym GRACE (God's Riches at Christ's Expense).

Chapter 7
Jesus Speaks and Stands for Us

1 John 2:1–6 (KJV)

My little children, these things write I unto you, that ye sin not. And if any man sin, we have an advocate with the Father, Jesus Christ the righteous:

And he is the propitiation for our sins: and not for ours only, but also for *the sins of* the whole world.

And hereby we do know that we know him, if we keep his commandments.

He that saith, I know him, and keepeth not his commandments, is a liar, and the truth is not in him.

But whoso keepeth his word, in him verily is the love of God perfected: hereby know we that we are in him.

He that saith he abideth in him ought himself also so to walk, even as he walked.

Saints are to live according to the Word of the Lord, so they will not sin. Believers are encouraged not to sin and certainly not to make it a habit. The aim of the saints is to please the Lord, and they do that by living a righteous life. John points out that the saints have someone to stand in their behalf in the event that they sin. The only way for man to be cleansed from his sin is through a righteous advocate stepping in, and Jesus Christ is the only one. When the believer messes up, he has Jesus, who is with the Father, speaking on his behalf. Jesus Christ is not only the advocate but He is also the propitiation; that is, He appeased the God of glory. One can put it like this: He is my advocate. He pleads my case, and He is my propitiation. He took my place.

Since Jesus has stood in for the saint, it becomes his responsibility to live in obedience to the commands of the Lord. When one has experienced the power and presence of the Lord in his heart and life, he will aim to please Him on a daily basis. There will be a real expression of the love of God in a believer's life as the result of obedience to the Word. As much as a saint desires to walk in the right direction according to the Word, he sometimes fails but he must not forget that he is not alone. The Holy Spirit is here, abiding in the heart of the saint, and Jesus Christ is at the right hand of the Father in heaven interceding on his behalf. Allstate insurance company claims that you are in good hands and fully covered with them, but real coverage is with the Lord God. The believer has coverage: the Holy Spirit on earth and is covered in heaven by the Son of God. Therefore, one is in the greatest hands of all times.

Chapter 8
Jesus, the Faithful High Priest

Hebrews 3:1–6 (KJV)

Wherefore, holy brethren, partakers of the heavenly calling, consider the Apostle and High Priest of our profession, Christ Jesus;

Who was faithful to him that appointed him, as also Moses *was faithful* in all his house.

For this *man* was counted worthy of more glory than Moses, inasmuch as he who hath builded the house hath more honour than the house.

For every house is builded by some *man;* but he that built all things *is* God.

And Moses verily *was* faithful in all his house, as a servant for a testimony of those things which were to be spoken after;

But Christ as a son over his own house; whose house are we, if we hold fast the confidence and the rejoicing of the hope firm unto the end.

*J*esus Christ is not only the Savior but He is the High Priest for all believers. The priest of the Old Testament times would go the Father on the behalf of the people. He had to offer up sacrifices for the sins of the people and his own sins. He would go into the holy of holies once a year to offer a sacrifice for the sins of all. The high priest was to serve faithfully, and he did, yet he was sinful himself. There was at least one big problem with all the priests that served; they could only serve until their deaths. They all died, and after their deaths, they were done.

Jesus Christ is the only hundred-percent faithful High Priest for He has been serving ever since going back to heaven to be with the Father. While Jesus was here on earth, He served as the Prophet for He led fallen man to have a relationship with the Heavenly Father. It is clearly pointed out in John 14:6 that Jesus is the only Way to the Father. Jesus was faithful to the task that the Father sent Him to do. He came to give His life on the cross of Calvary, and He did that and rose from the dead. After Christ completed His mission on earth, He went back to the Father where He sat down on the right hand of the Father. All saints must understand that Jesus is very active in heaven for He is serving as their High Priest.

Chapter 9
Our Lord Prayed in Pain

Luke 22:39–46 (KJV)

And he came out, and went, as he was wont, to the mount of Olives; and his disciples also followed him.

And when he was at the place, he said unto them, Pray that ye enter not into temptation.

And he was withdrawn from them about a stone's cast, and kneeled down, and prayed,

Saying, Father, if thou be willing, remove this cup from me: nevertheless not my will, but thine, be done.

And there appeared an angel unto him from heaven, strengthening him.

And being in an agony he prayed more earnestly: and his sweat was as it were great drops of blood falling down to the ground.

And when he rose up from prayer, and was come to his disciples, he found them sleeping for sorrow,

And said unto them, Why sleep ye? rise and pray, lest ye enter into temptation.

Jesus was on His way to the cross to die for the sins of the world. However, before He was to give His life for mankind, He spent some time with His disciples. Before the prayer in the garden, He had been with the disciples in the upper room to keep the Passover and to institute the Lord's Supper. Jesus and the eleven disciples left the upper room and went to the Garden of Gethsemane. He left eight of the eleven disciples at the gate of the garden and took three into the garden with Him as He was getting ready to pray. Jesus went a little distance from them to be alone with His Father in prayer. He told the three to watch and pray, but they went to sleep.

Jesus prayed for the passing of the cup. What was in the cup? The sins of the world were in the cup, and drinking the cup meant that He would be separated from the Father. It was not that Jesus was trying to get out of dying for fallen humanity, but for the first time He would not have fellowship with the Father. He was heading to the moment of being forsaken by the Father (Psalm 22:1; Matthew 27:46; Mark 15:34). In His praying, He sweated so that it looked like great drops of blood. This is what one would call hard praying. Jesus moved to the "nevertheless" point in His prayer for He wanted to do His Father's will as He had done all through His earthly life. Jesus was willing to lose a moment of fellowship with the Father, so mankind could have eternity with Him and the Father.

Chapter 10
Be Thankful to the Lord

Psalm 107:1–15 (KJV)

O give thanks unto the LORD for *he is* good:
for his mercy *endureth* for ever.

Let the redeemed of the LORD say *so*, whom
he hath redeemed from the hand of the enemy;

And gathered them out of the lands, from the
east, and from the west, from the north, and
from the south.

They wandered in the wilderness in a solitary way; they found no city to dwell in.

Hungry and thirsty, their soul fainted in them.

Then they cried unto the LORD in their trouble, *and* he delivered them out of their distresses.

And he led them forth by the right way, that they might go to a city of habitation.

Oh that *men* would praise the LORD *for* his goodness, and *for* his wonderful works to the children of men!

For he satisfieth the longing soul, and filleth the hungry soul with goodness.

Such as sit in darkness and in the shadow of death, *being* bound in affliction and iron;

Because they rebelled against the words of God, and contemned the counsel of the most High:

53

Therefore he brought down their heart with labour; they fell down, and *there was* none to help.

Then they cried unto the LORD in their trouble, *and* he saved them out of their distresses.

He brought them out of darkness and the shadow of death, and brake their bands in sunder.

Oh that *men* would praise the LORD *for* his goodness, and *for* his wonderful works to the children of men!

Saints ought to spend time giving thanks to the Lord, not just on Thanksgiving Day, but all year long. If believers would start thanking the Lord more for all things, the good and the bad, they would have less time to complain about life. When one stops and thinks about what the Lord has done over his life, he will discover that he has more to be thankful for than he thought. In this Psalm, God's people are told to give thanks for His goodness. God had expressed His goodness in many ways to Israel as they were in Egypt and in the wilderness. He brought them out of Egypt and cared for them in the wilderness. When they did not have the necessities of life, such as water and food, they cried to the Lord, and He provided for them. They were to be thankful for how God had protected and delivered them from the hands of the enemy.

The cry is made that men are to praise the Lord for His goodness. How good is the Lord to you? Can you count your blessings? Can you name your blessings? Why not try to name and count the blessings, and you will realize how blessed you are. I heard a story a long time ago from a great preacher that I knew.He said, "Two men were talking about asking the Lord for things and one man said that he had not asked the Lord for anything in fourteen years." The other man said, "There is no way anyone can go that long and not ask the Lord for something." The first man said, "Yes it is. See I have just been thanking the Lord every day and by the time I thank Him, He has blessed me with something else." All saints are to show the Lord appreciation for all that He does. As you go through each day, why not just thank the Lord for His goodness

Chapter 11

Seeking the Lord for a Better Day

Zechariah 8:18–23 (KJV)

And the word of the LORD of hosts came unto me, saying,

Thus saith the LORD of hosts; The fast of the fourth *month,* and the fast of the fifth, and the fast of the seventh, and the fast of the tenth, shall be to the house of Judah joy and gladness, and cheerful feasts; therefore love the truth and peace.

Thus saith the LORD of hosts; *It shall* yet *come to pass,* that there shall come people, and the inhabitants of many cities:

And the inhabitants of one *city* shall go to another, saying, Let us go speedily to pray before the LORD, and to seek the LORD of hosts: I will go also.

Yea, many people and strong nations shall come to seek the LORD of hosts in Jerusalem, and to pray before the LORD.

Thus saith the LORD of hosts; In those days *it shall come to pass,* that ten men shall take hold out of all languages of the nations, even shall take hold of the skirt of him that is a Jew, saying, We will go with you: for we have heard *that* God *is* with you.

This passage deals with the end times which will be after the Rapture of the saved and the Great Tribulation Period. This passage is speaking of the Millennial Reign of Christ on earth. The day is coming when Jesus Christ will sit on His throne and rule the earth. There will be peace in the valley for the Lord will bring about a peaceful period for mankind. He will turn all of the fasts of each month into a joyful and cheerful moment for all His people. The word of Judah's joy and peace will reach all over the world, and people from other countries will travel to find out how they can have it, too. They will be seeking the God of Abraham. The word would have reached them that the

Lord gives peace and gladness to all who seek Him for themselves. They will never be the same because the presence of the Lord will be in their lives.

Why couldn't believers have such a day now so that people from all over our towns, cities, counties, states, nations, and the world come seeking the Lord? If saints in our churches were real in their worship and witness for Jesus Christ, people would be coming from all over seeking the Lord. When one has been converted by the Holy Spirit to accept Jesus Christ as Lord and Savior, there is no way for him or her to stay quiet about the peace that He gives. Saints are to lift the name of Jesus everywhere they go for His name draws people from all nations. It would be wonderful if people came seeking the Lord's favor in our churches today. To seek His favor is to abide in Him and His Word; it is rewarding to seek the Lord (Hebrews 11:6). God gives power and strength to all who seek His favor.

Are you seeking the Lord's favor? If so, how are you seeking His favor? Why are you seeking His favor? Do you want to be known, or do you want others to know the Lord?

Chapter 12
Asking Someone to Pray for You

Jeremiah 42:1–6 (KJV)

Then all the captains of the forces, and Johanan
the son of Kareah, and Jezaniah the son of
Hoshaiah, and all the people from the least even
unto the greatest, came near,

And said unto Jeremiah the prophet, Let, we
beseech thee, our supplication be accepted
before thee, and pray for us unto the LORD thy

God, *even* for all this remnant; (for we are left *but* a few of many, as thine eyes do behold us:) That the LORD thy God may shew us the way wherein we may walk, and the thing that we may do.

Then Jeremiah the prophet said unto them, I have heard *you;* behold, I will pray unto the LORD your God according to your words; and it shall come to pass, *that* whatsoever thing the LORD shall answer you, I will declare *it* unto you; I will keep nothing back from you.

Then they said to Jeremiah, The LORD be a true and faithful witness between us, if we do not even according to all things for the which the LORD thy God shall send thee to us.

Whether *it be* good, or whether *it be* evil, we will obey the voice of the LORD our God, to whom we send thee; that it may be well with us, when we obey the voice of the LORD our God.

*T*he leaders over the people, Johanan and Jezaniah, were concerned about the people's spiritual welfare. They along with others went to the prophet of the Lord, Jeremiah, asking him to pray for them. There are times in a believer's life that he needs someone else to call on the Lord in his behalf. They were seeking directions from the Lord, so they could go in the right way. All saints ought to make sure that they are going in the right direction, and in being sure, sometimes they need someone to approach the throne of God for them. The people who came to Jeremiah had a heart and mind to be obedient.

Jeremiah had a listening ear to hear the people's concern, and this is what a believer must have if he is going to pray for someone. There are too many who say they will pray for someone, but they do not listen to their need. In order to properly pray for someone, you need to properly listen first as Jeremiah did. He also prayed according to the people's words to the Lord. Since you are asked to pray, be careful not to change one's concerns. Believers must keep in mind that the answer to prayer is in the Lord. Jeremiah told them that he would give the Lord's answer to them, whatever it was. When saints pray for others after being asked, they are to give the answer the Lord has given them if it is to be shared.

The people knew that the Lord of Jeremiah was true and faithful, and therefore, they were willing to accept and obey the answer. They knew that it pays to obey the voice of the Lord. The saints in today's world should be willing to accept and obey the Lord's voice. It is not enough to ask for prayer and get the answer, but obedience to the Lord is a must if one wants to be blessed.

Are you asking someone to pray about a need? Are you being direct in your request? Are you willing to accept the answer, whatever it is? Do you have a heart to obey the Lord?

Chapter 13
Prayers Are Made for You

2 Thessalonians 1:5–12 (KJV)

Which is a manifest token of the righteous judg-ment of God, that ye may be counted worthy of the kingdom of God for which ye also suffer: Seeing *it is* a righteous thing with God to rec-ompense tribulation to them that trouble you;

And to you who are troubled rest with us, when the Lord Jesus shall be revealed from heaven with his mighty angels,

In flaming fire taking vengeance on them that know not God, and that obey not the gospel of our Lord Jesus Christ:

Who shall be punished with everlasting destruction from the presence of the Lord, and from the glory of his power;

When he shall come to be glorified in his saints, and to be admired in all them that believe (because our testimony among you was believed) in that day.

Wherefore also we pray always for you, that our God would count you worthy of *this* calling, and

fulfil all the good pleasure of *his* goodness, and
the work of faith with power:
That the name of our Lord Jesus Christ may be
glorified in you, and ye in him, according to the
grace of our God and the Lord Jesus Christ.

*P*aul is saying to the believers in Thessalonica
that God has the final say about those who
are mistreating His people. The day is coming when
the Lord will put a stop to suffering of His people by
the hand of the enemies of the Cross of Christ. Paul
also let them know directly and believers today indi-
rectly that things will get worse before they get better.
This passage is speaking of the final days of the Great
Tribulation Period when the Lord Jesus Christ comes
with His saints to take vengeance in His own hands. He

will execute judgment on all who have not believed and accepted His finished work on the cross for man's sins. These people will be cast into the lake of fire, which is the second death (Revelation 20), and they will be forever out of the presence of God Almighty.

Paul made known that the saints were in his prayers. It is always great to know that believers are being prayed for by other saints. Saints that are real in their concerns for others. Paul wanted to encourage the Thessalonians in the midst of their pains and sufferings for the cause of Christ. When the Lord looks at the sufferings of His people for the cause of Christ, they are counted worthy. The more the devil tries to destroy the people of God, the more Christ's name is glorified. When saints are lifted up in prayer by other saints, they can make it through whatever they are facing. Saints rest in the fact that the end will be better than what they are going through right now because the Lord is giving them grace.

Who are you praying for? Why are you praying for them? Do you expect the Lord to answer your prayers? Do you desire others to find rest in knowing that the Lord will have the final word?

Chapter 14
Knowing God Will Hear and Answer

Lamentations 3:52–58 (KJV)

Mine enemies chased me sore, like a bird, without cause.

They have cut off my life in the dungeon, and cast a stone upon me.

Waters flowed over mine head; *then* I said, I am cut off.

I called upon thy name, O LORD, out of the low dungeon.

Thou hast heard my voice: hide not thine ear at my breathing, at my cry.

Thou drewest near in the day *that* I called upon thee: thou saidst, Fear not.

O Lord, thou hast pleaded the causes of my soul; thou hast redeemed my life.

*D*oes God hear and answer prayers? Many people ask that question every day. The pressures of life can be so rough that one thinks he can't make it any longer. He is at the end of the road and doesn't know which way to go. All he can see is the enemy coming toward him to take him out, but then, from within, he cries out to the Lord of glory. The Holy

Spirit reminds a believer that his strength is in the Lord, and he can count on Him to be present to help at all times. It is a great thing to know that you can trust the Lord in the time of troubles, and He will be there.

Now the truth of the matter is a saint should not wait until trouble comes to call on the Lord. As a parent of a grown son or daughter, would it be okay with you if he or she only called you when he or she is in trouble? Most parents that I know want to have a great relationship and fellowship with their grown children. If there is a great relationship between parent and grown son and daughter, it would not be a problem if he or she called the parent when trouble comes. When saints have a great relationship and fellowship with the Lord, they know that it would not be a problem to call on Him when trouble comes. It is great to live with the knowledge that God does hear and answer the prayers of His people. Are you trusting the Lord? Do you have a great relationship with the Lord? How often do you call on the Lord? Do you know for a fact that God hears and answers prayers? Why not call on the Lord when all is well?

Chapter 15
Always Pray for You
1 Samuel 12:19–25 (KJV)

And all the people said unto Samuel, Pray for thy servants unto the LORD thy God, that we die not: for we have added unto all our sins *this* evil, to ask us a king.

And Samuel said unto the people, Fear not: ye have done all this wickedness: yet turn not aside from following the LORD, but serve the LORD with all your heart;

And turn ye not aside: for *then should ye go* after vain *things,* which cannot profit nor deliver; for they *are* vain.

For the LORD will not forsake his people for his great name's sake: because it hath pleased the LORD to make you his people.

Moreover as for me, God forbid that I should sin against the LORD in ceasing to pray for you: but I will teach you the good and the right way:

Only fear the LORD, and serve him in truth with all your heart: for consider how great *things* he hath done for you.

But if ye shall still do wickedly, ye shall be consumed, both ye and your king.

*P*lease note that Israel had asked for a king like other countries. God had given them what they had asked for, but now they were crying because of the way King Saul was treating them. They realized that they had sinned against the Lord by asking for a king. In the tough spot, they knew who to go to for help; the prophet Samuel was there for them. They desired Samuel to pray for them because they thought death was on its way. He made known to them that they had done wrong, but the Lord was not getting ready to destroy them. Samuel lifted up one thing to them that they kept; they continued to serve the Lord with all their hearts. He assured them that God would not forsake them for His name's sake. Saints can always keep in mind that the Lord will not mess up His own name.

Take note that Samuel considered it a sin to stop praying for the people of God. The pastors who are over the people of God must always be mindful of the fact that they must pray for the people. It is a great duty of the ministers. However, all saints ought to pray for others regularly. He also points out that while I am praying for you, I will also teach you what the Lord expects of you. The Lord does desire His people to respect and serve Him with a true heart and with thanksgiving for all His blessings. There are many blessings that the Lord has for His people, and they will receive them if they live in His will. Samuel also let Israel know that if they chose to keep doing wickedly, they would be cut off. It is much better to live in the will of the Lord and receive His blessings.

Have you ever prayed for anything that you regretted later? Has the Lord given you what you wanted? Are you praying for anyone always? Is there anyone praying for you always? Is there a need for constant prayer for you? Why is it important for someone to stay in prayer for you?

Chapter 16
Draw Me Closer, Lord

Psalm 69:4–18 (KJV)

They that hate me without a cause are more than the hairs of mine head: they that would destroy me, *being* mine enemies wrongfully, are mighty: then I restored *that* which I took not away.

O God, thou knowest my foolishness; and my sins are not hid from thee.

Let not them that wait on thee, O Lord GOD of hosts, be ashamed for my sake: let not those that seek thee be confounded for my sake, O God of Israel.

Because for thy sake I have borne reproach; shame hath covered my face.

I am become a stranger unto my brethren, and an alien unto my mother's children.

For the zeal of thine house hath eaten me up; and the reproaches of them that reproached thee are fallen upon me.

When I wept, *and chastened* my soul with fasting, that was to my reproach.

I made sackcloth also my garment; and I became a proverb to them.

They that sit in the gate speak against me; and I *was* the song of the drunkards.

But as for me, my prayer *is* unto thee, O LORD, *in* an acceptable time: O God, in the multitude of thy mercy hear me, in the truth of thy salvation. Deliver me out of the mire, and let me not sink: let me be delivered from them that hate me, and out of the deep waters.

Let not the waterflood overflow me, neither let the deep swallow me up, and let not the pit shut her mouth upon me.

Hear me, O LORD; for thy lovingkindness *is* good: turn unto me according to the multitude of thy tender mercies.

And hide not thy face from thy servant; for I am in trouble: hear me speedily.

Draw nigh unto my soul, *and* redeem it: deliver me because of mine enemies.

*T*he Psalmist was in trouble, and he knew who to call on for help. He acknowledged his own unwise moves in life, and he knew that they were not hidden from the Lord. He felt very bad because of his actions, and he had been turned away from his own family. He realized that he was the laughingstock of those of the streets. Saints must know that when they do not live up to the standard of the Lord, they are the talk of the town in a bad manner. Believers can't live just any kind of way and expect the world to think well of them.

He cried out to the Lord in the moment of life that he was down and out. He knew that the mercies of the

Lord were available to all who call on Him for He hears the cries of His people. If you are going through a rough period of life, stop and call on the Lord for He cares for you (1 Peter 5:7). The world can ride over you to no end, and you can be at the end of the road, not knowing that help is only a call away. The Holy Spirit lives in all saints, and He will lead them to the One who can help in their hour of despair. The Lord cares for His people better than a loving mother does her children. There are some great mothers who love and care for their children and will do everything in the world for them. Their expressions of love are only because of the love of the Lord in their hearts. As you think about a mother's love, think on the Lord's loving kindness toward His people.

Believers are to depend on the Lord to be present for them in the time of trouble. He will not leave them hanging out to dry for He cares for them. God the Father, through His Son by the Holy Spirit, will protect saints from the hands of the enemies and keep them in a safe place.

Are you asking the Lord to draw near to you? Do you really want the Lord near? Do you understand that if the Lord is near, your life will not be the same?

Chapter 17
Depend on the Lord

Psalm 102:21–27 (KJV)

To declare the name of the LORD in Zion, and his praise in Jerusalem;

When the people are gathered together, and the kingdoms, to serve the LORD.

He weakened my strength in the way; he shortened my days.

I said, O my God, take me not away in the midst of my days: thy years *are* throughout all generations.

Of old hast thou laid the foundation of the earth: and the heavens *are* the work of thy hands.

They shall perish, but thou shalt endure: yea, all of them shall wax old like a garment; as a vesture shalt thou change them, and they shall be changed:

But thou *art* the same, and thy years shall have no end.

*W*hile you are telling others about the Lord and praising Him for all that He does, keep in mind that your days are coming to a close. Since all believers' days are coming to an end, it is of great importance to tell people everywhere that God is real. We all can see people from all walks of life coming to the Lord and worshipping Him, and at the same time we are getting older and weaker. The Psalmist tells that his own strength for his body is not as powerful as it once was for he had ministered to others. When you have been about serving the Lord, your physical strength leaves you at times. Therefore, all saints must know the source of their strength (Psalm 27:1). He cried out to the Lord for help in midst of his days. The Lord is the only one that can renew strength and give power to continue when one is worn.

Believers are to keep in mind that the Lord laid the foundation of this earth and has maintained it all these years. Since He has done that, one ought not to doubt His ability to keep us in the midst of all life storms.

People and things are perishing every day, but the Lord is the same for He can't change (Malachi 3:6). He is just as strong today as He was in the days of Adam and Eve. Now that you know God has the strength you need for the journeys of life, trust Him with your whole being. Learn to cry out to Him for help for He is closer than all others you have been calling. You can call for help from family, friends, pastor, church, and others, and all could be out of reach. It does not matter what cell phone services one uses; all companies have problems at times. However, the Lord has given His people a hookup that never has a problem. Call Him up; call Him up and tell Him what you want.

Who do you call on in time of trouble? Have you called the Lord? Do you believe He will hear and answer? Has He ever helped you out of any trouble?

Chapter 18
Humility is the Way before God

Luke 18:9–14 (KJV)

And he spake this parable unto certain which
trusted in themselves that they were righteous,
and despised others:

Two men went up into the temple to pray; the
one a Pharisee, and the other a publican.

The Pharisee stood and prayed thus with himself, God, I thank thee, that I am not as other

men *are,* extortioners, unjust, adulterers, or even as this publican.

I fast twice in the week, I give tithes of all that I possess.

And the publican, standing afar off, would not lift up so much as *his* eyes unto heaven, but smote upon his breast, saying, God be merciful to me a sinner.

I tell you, this man went down to his house justified *rather* than the other: for every one that exalteth himself shall be abased; and he that humbleth himself shall be exalted.

*S*aints are to be very careful how they come before the Father. They are not to approach the Father in a manner as though He owes them something. God is the Father of all saints, and He desires to be approached in a humble way. When one goes to the Father in the same manner as the Pharisee did, he is considered to be self-righteous. Jesus talks about two men that went to the temple to pray. There was a Pharisee who was self-centered; everything was about him and what he did. Then there was a publican who was not much in his own eyes and in the eyes of the Pharisee. However, he had the right spirit. He came in the temple in the right manner and prayed a very humble prayer. He asked the Lord to be merciful to him as a sinner. Now this is what you will call a humble spirit.

Jesus gives an update report on the humble man. He said that the publican went home justified; that is, he was made right with the Father in heaven. Christ taught that if one wants to be lifted up, he must take the low seat. The way up is down; to become important is to be the least, and to be master is to serve. Jesus Christ is the example of real humility (John 13). He washed the feet of the disciples, teaching them that the Lord is a servant. Saints must never think that they are too important to serve others and in certain positions. The Lord is looking for people with towels and bowls of water, ready to serve others instead of those with titles and seats, waiting to be served.

How humble are you? Can the Lord count on you to serve others? What kind of spirit do you have? Are you looking at yourself or in self? What does the Lord observe about your humility?

Chapter 19
God's People Humble Themselves

2 Chronicles 7:11–18 (KJV)

Thus Solomon finished the house of the LORD, and the king's house: and all that came into Solomon's heart to make in the house of the LORD, and in his own house, he prosperously effected.

And the LORD appeared to Solomon by night, and said unto him, I have heard thy prayer, and have chosen this place to myself for an house of sacrifice.

If I shut up heaven that there be no rain, or if I command the locusts to devour the land, or if I send pestilence among my people;

If my people, which are called by my name, shall humble themselves, and pray, and seek my face, and turn from their wicked ways; then will I hear from heaven, and will forgive their sin, and will heal their land.

Now mine eyes shall be open, and mine ears attend unto the prayer *that is made* in this place. For now have I chosen and sanctified this house, that my name may be there for ever: and mine eyes and mine heart shall be there perpetually.

And as for thee, if thou wilt walk before me, as David thy father walked, and do according to all that I have commanded thee, and shalt observe my statutes and my judgments;

Then will I stablish the throne of thy kingdom, according as I have covenanted with David thy father, saying, There shall not fail thee a man *to be* ruler in Israel.

Solomon completed building both houses and prayed a dedicated prayer to the Lord. You will find his prayer in 2 Chronicles chapter six, and there are many "ifs," but here the Lord answers Solomon. He let him know that He had heard his prayer and had chosen this place for His name, His eyes, His ears, and His heart forever. The Lord is everywhere, and saints

97

ought to be able to feel His presence everywhere they go. However, one needs to pay attention to the fact that the Lord has said that He will be present in His house as He promised. Since God will be in His house and you are His child, why not go to His house to be with Him?

The Lord tells Solomon that he is to live in the same manner of his father David. He was to live in obedience to the commands and observe the statutes and judgments of God if he wanted his kingdom to be established and to continue. There are too many believers who want the blessings of God but do not live in obedience to the commands of God. He expects saints to walk the walk as well as talk the talk. It is not enough for saints to talk about the Lord but not do what He says.

Please note in verses thirteen and fourteen, the Lord says that if He shut up, command and send these things to His people then His people have a great task to carry out. There are many believers who know verse fourteen by heart and can tell this promise in a heartbeat. God's people are marked by His name and are to do four things if they want to claim this promise. They are to humble themselves, pray, seek God's face, and turn from their wicked ways. Then the Lord will hear, forgive, and heal. The problem comes with saints not carrying out their part; yet they expect the Lord to do His part. Believers must have a humble spirit and always be willing to submit to the Lord.

Are you humbling yourself before God? Are you willing to carry out your part of the promise?

Chapter 20
Getting Things Right before God

2 Chronicles 34:24–33 (KJV)

Thus saith the LORD, Behold, I will bring evil upon this place, and upon the inhabitants thereof, *even* all the curses that are written in the book which they have read before the king of Judah:

Because they have forsaken me, and have burned incense unto other gods, that they might provoke me to anger with all the works of their hands; therefore my wrath shall be poured out upon this place, and shall not be quenched.

And as for the king of Judah, who sent you to enquire of the LORD, so shall ye say unto him, Thus saith the LORD God of Israel *concerning* the words which thou hast heard;

Because thine heart was tender, and thou didst humble thyself before God, when thou heardest his words against this place, and against the inhabitants thereof, and humbledst thyself before me, and didst rend thy clothes, and weep before me; I have even heard *thee* also, saith the LORD.

Behold, I will gather thee to thy fathers, and thou shalt be gathered to thy grave in peace, neither shall thine eyes see all the evil that I will bring upon this place, and upon the inhabitants of the same. So they brought the king word again.

Then the king sent and gathered together all the elders of Judah and Jerusalem.

And the king went up into the house of the LORD, and all the men of Judah, and the inhabitants of Jerusalem, and the priests, and the Levites, and all the people, great and small: and he read in their ears all the words of the book of the covenant that was found in the house of the LORD.

And the king stood in his place, and made a covenant before the LORD, to walk after the LORD, and to keep his commandments, and his

testimonies, and his statutes, with all his heart,
and with all his soul, to perform the words of the
covenant which are written in this book.

And he caused all that were present in Jerusalem
and Benjamin to stand *to it*. And the inhabitants
of Jerusalem did according to the covenant of
God, the God of their fathers.

And Josiah took away all the abominations out
of all the countries that *pertained* to the children
of Israel, and made all that were present in Israel
to serve, *even* to serve the LORD their God. *And*
all his days they departed not from following
the LORD, the God of their fathers.

*W*hen things are not going right in your life,
stop and look at your actions. It could be

that you have turned away from the instructions of the Lord and are not following after His will. Josiah the king was concerned about the condition of Israel to the point that he wanted to know the real problem. So he sent a group to Huldah to find out from her what the Lord had to say. They brought word back to the king, saying the real problem is that Israel had left the Lord God and His ways. Israel was heading for a great downfall, but the Lord saw the humble spirit of King Josiah. When the leader has a humble spirit, it will not go unnoticed by the Lord. The Lord rewards those who have a humble spirit. The king made an open commitment to the Lord and His words. He also led the people to make the same commitment. Therefore, they had the promise of the Lord that He would blessed their obedience. Josiah the king got rid of all the false things that

Israel had brought into the daily operations; after a commitment to walk right, there must be action.

It is every saint's responsibility to humble themselves before the Lord. God is to be recognized for who He is and not be taken lightly. Christians must have the right spirit when going before the Lord. They are not to go before the Lord in the attitude of Cain for he went in a careless manner. Jesus gave mankind the greatest example of going before the Father in the Garden of Gethsemane for He fell on His face (Matthew 26:39) and prayed to the Father in heaven. Here one can see that Jesus had a humble spirit. Jesus is God in human flesh, and yet He went before His Father every time in a humble manner. This is what all believers are to do, regardless of the position they may serve in, for none are on the level of God.

Are you humbling yourself before God? What kind of spirit do you have? What do you do when things are not right in your life? What is your reaction when you are told that you are wrong?

Chapter 21
A Real Challenge to Be Perfect

Matthew 19:16–22 (KJV)

And, behold, one came and said unto him, Good Master, what good thing shall I do, that I may have eternal life?

And he said unto him, Why callest thou me good? *there is* none good but one, *that is,* God: but if thou wilt enter into life, keep the commandments.

He saith unto him, Which? Jesus said, Thou shalt do no murder, Thou shalt not commit adultery, Thou shalt not steal, Thou shalt not bear false witness,

Honour thy father and *thy* mother: and, Thou shalt love thy neighbour as thyself.

The young man saith unto him, All these things have I kept from my youth up: what lack I yet?

Jesus said unto him, If thou wilt be perfect, go *and* sell that thou hast, and give to the poor, and thou shalt have treasure in heaven: and come *and* follow me.

But when the young man heard that saying, he went away sorrowful: for he had great possessions.

One may have in his mind that he has to do something in order to get eternal life; however, man cannot earn eternal life by his actions. There are many people who believe if they do good deeds, it will get them a ticket into heaven. If heaven is obtained by good deeds, how much does one have to do? The young man addressed Jesus as Good Master, but Jesus pointed out to him that the only one good is God. Jesus was letting him know that if he really knew God, then he would know who He is, and His purpose of coming was to give eternal life. However, he thought that he could work his way into favor with the Lord. In other words, Jesus says since you want to do something, keep the commandments. He asked Jesus which one, and He gave him a list of commandments to be kept. He claimed that he had done that and then wanted to know what else.

Jesus gives the real test, a test that really hit his heart and made him think. Jesus tells him since you want to do something here it is, sell and give to the ones in need and come follow Me. Jesus was not saying by selling and giving that one is saved. He was pointing out that it is a perfect act. Jesus knew where his heart was; he trusted in his riches. This real test will cause a man to think about where he is and what he has. What he had was more important to him than eternal life for he left Jesus without accepting Him. The only way for one to become perfect is through the blood of Jesus. Eternal life is available, and one can receive it by believing in Jesus Christ and His finished work on the cross.

Do you want to be perfect? Will you part with things that are dear to you? Are you willing to give to help others? Do you trust in your stuff? Are you willing to place your trust in Jesus Christ? Do you believe perfection in only in Jesus Christ?

Chapter 22
Let Mercy Override Judgement
James 2:8–13 (KJV)

If ye fulfil the royal law according to the scripture, Thou shalt love thy neighbour as thyself, ye do well:

But if ye have respect to persons, ye commit sin, and are convinced of the law as transgressors.

For whosoever shall keep the whole law, and yet offend in one *point,* he is guilty of all.

For he that said, Do not commit adultery, said also, Do not kill. Now if thou commit no adultery, yet if thou kill, thou art become a transgressor of the law.

So speak ye, and so do, as they that shall be judged by the law of liberty.

For he shall have judgment without mercy, that hath shewed no mercy; and mercy rejoiceth against judgment.

The best expression of keeping the law is loving and treating others like you love and treat yourself. The Lord expects saints to have His love in their hearts and to move it out through their hearts to people. This love is to be for everybody, and believers are not to pick and choose whom they will love. There is a wrong kind of respect, which is when one shows kindness to some and not to others just because they are not of them. Jesus taught His disciples that they are to love as He loves. All saints know that Jesus Christ loves everybody. He expressed the Father's love to all; it did not matter to Him who they were or where they came from.

Be careful of anyone who claims to be obedient to the whole law. He will brag about doing this and that as if he is not guilty of breaking the law. James makes it clear that if one messes up in one point, he has broken the law. Therefore, when it is put before believers in this manner, they cannot point their finger at one person for doing this thing and not point at the other for doing that; both are guilty of breaking the law. In a court of law, each one would be found a transgressor for both had sinned. Believers must keep in mind that if they judge others without mercy, they will be judged without mercy. The Bible does not teach that saints are not to judge at all, but it teaches that they are to judge righteously. Saints ought to use mercy as a rule in judging for it is to override the judgment. When mercy is displayed toward others, rejoicing will take place in both parties. If all saints judge with mercy as the Lord who has been merciful toward them, there will be more rejoicing in the world.

How do you judge? Do you judge as you want to be judged? Where is mercy in your judging toward love others? Do you express love toward others? Do you have any rejoicing in your life?

Chapter 23
Obey the Leader's Commands

Joshua 22:1–6 (KJV)

Then Joshua called the Reubenites, and the Gadites, and the half tribe of Manasseh,

And said unto them, Ye have kept all that Moses the servant of the LORD commanded you, and have obeyed my voice in all that I commanded you:

Ye have not left your brethren these many days unto this day, but have kept the charge of the commandment of the LORD your God.

And now the LORD your God hath given rest unto your brethren, as he promised them: therefore now return ye, and get you unto your tents, *and* unto the land of your possession, which Moses the servant of the LORD gave you on the other side Jordan.

But take diligent heed to do the commandment and the law, which Moses the servant of the LORD charged you, to love the LORD your God, and to walk in all his ways, and to keep his commandments, and to cleave unto him, and to serve him with all your heart and with all your soul.

117

So Joshua blessed them, and sent them away: and they went unto their tents.

*T*he Children of Israel had crossed the Jordan and entered into the Promised Land. The Lord had blessed Joshua to follow Moses in leading Israel. Moses was able to lead them within sight of the Promised Land but not into it. The Lord commanded Moses to prepare Joshua to lead Israel after his death. Before the death of Moses, it was made known that each tribe would be given lands in the Promised Land on the other side of Jordan except the tribes of Reuben, Gad, and half of Manasseh. They desired lands on the East side of Jordan and were given their lands before all others. They were instructed by Moses to go with their brothers to fight the battles in order to obtain the

118

Promised Land. The tribes of Reuben, Gad, and half Manasseh faithfully kept their words and obeyed the instructions of Moses. When the Promised Land was conquered, they were allowed to go back over the Jordan to their lands and rest as the other tribes were resting now in the Promised Land.

There are lessons for all saints could to learn from the tribes of Reuben, Gad, and half of Manasseh.

1. Make your request known to the leader that the Lord has over you.

2. Listen to the voice of the leader that the Lord has over you.

3. Keep the commands of the leader that the Lord has over you.

4. Obey the voice of the next leader that the Lord has over you.

5. Don't forget the laws and commands of the Lord.

6. Love God.

7. Walk in God's ways.

8. Keep the Lord's commands.

9. Serve the Lord with your whole being.

All believers will be blessed by the Lord with special blessings when He is obeyed. Are you following the instructions of the Lord that the Lord's servant has given you? Do you serve the Lord with a sincere heart? Have you recognized the blessings of the Lord in your life of obedience?

Chapter 24
Looking out for Others

Philippians 2:1–5 (KJV)

If *there be* therefore any consolation in Christ, if any comfort of love, if any fellowship of the Spirit, if any bowels and mercies,

Fulfil ye my joy, that ye be likeminded, having the same love, *being* of one accord, of one mind.

Let nothing *be done* through strife or vainglory; but in lowliness of mind let each esteem other better than themselves.

Look not every man on his own things, but every man also on the things of others.

Let this mind be in you, which was also in Christ Jesus:

*S*aints are to live according to the glory of the Lord, and one way to that is to be concerned about others. The Lord does not want believers to go through life just concerned about themselves. He has saved them so they can be a blessing to others. Each day that the Holy Spirt wakes all believers up is another day to find consolation, comfort, fellowship, compassion, and mercies that have been given to them. As the

122

Lord has given you all the elements aforementioned, it is your Christian responsibility to share those same elements to others as He gives you opportunities. When believers' loved ones go home to be with the Lord they need comfort for it hurts; other saints are to be there to give that comfort. If all believers in any given church were united as one, caring for each other, just think how strong that church would be to the glory of the Lord. Unity is what the Lord desires to see in the church and among all saints everywhere.

Believers are to be very careful how they do what they do, making sure that it is done with the right spirit. If things are not done in the right spirit while helping others, the Lord is not glorified. It should always be the aim of all saints to do things in a manner that will bring glory to the Lord. Saints should encourage and lift others up to build them up in the Lord. Some people just need to be lifted because they have gone through things that have pulled them down. Therefore, be there for others that are going through things. Saints are to operate with the mind of Christ. Jesus has a serving mind. Jesus has a loving mind. Jesus has a caring mind. Jesus has a humble mind.

Are you concerned about others? Do you seek to encourage others? Are you lifting up others? Do you have the mind of Christ?

Chapter 25
The Greatest Commandment of All

Matthew 22:34–40 (KJV)

But when the Pharisees had heard that he had put the Sadducees to silence, they were gathered together.

Then one of them, *which was* a lawyer, asked *him a question,* tempting him, and saying,

Master, which *is* the great commandment in the law?

Jesus said unto him, Thou shalt love the Lord thy God with all thy heart, and with all thy soul, and with all thy mind.

This is the first and great commandment.

And the second *is* like unto it, Thou shalt love thy neighbour as thyself.

On these two commandments hang all the law and the prophets.

*T*here are always some people who think that they are better than others just because of who they are. These people are out to find fault with others just like the Pharisees and Sadducees. They were always trying to find fault in Jesus, but they were never successful for there is no fault in Jesus. They would ask questions of Jesus, attempting to see if He would go against the Law of Moses. So their question of the day was, "Which commandment is the greatest?" What they had in mind was the Ten Commandments. They were expecting Jesus to point out just one of the Commandments. Jesus took the Ten Commandments and wrapped them up into two commandments.

The first commandment is dealing with saints' relationship with God, and it covers the first four of the Ten Commandments. Believers are to love the Father with their whole being, and if they love Him as they should, His love will come out in their life each day. When one loves the Lord, he will have a great relationship with Him through Jesus Christ by the leading of the Holy Spirit. A great relationship will lead to a working fellowship. John talks about the fellowship with the Father and Jesus Christ (1 John 1). This commandment is the greatest because one can't carry out the second one properly without loving God right.

The second commandment is dealing with believers' relationships with one another, and it covers the last six of the Ten Commandments. Saints are to love others as they love themselves. When one loves himself, he will not harm himself. Therefore, he will not go about harming others. The Lord wants believers to love and treat each other with His love. There are at least twenty-six "one another" statements in the New Testament about how saints are to treat others.

Do you know the first and greatest commandment? Are you loving God right? Are you loving others right? Are you seeking to live in the love of God?

Chapter 26
Ready for the Lord's Coming

Matthew 24:37–44 (KJV)

But as the days of Noe *were*, so shall also the coming of the Son of man be.

For as in the days that were before the flood they were eating and drinking, marrying and giving in marriage, until the day that Noe entered into the ark,

And knew not until the flood came, and took them all away; so shall also the coming of the Son of man be.

Then shall two be in the field; the one shall be taken, and the other left.

Two *women shall be* grinding at the mill; the one shall be taken, and the other left.

Watch therefore: for ye know not what hour your Lord doth come.

But know this, that if the goodman of the house had known in what watch the thief would come, he would have watched, and would not have suffered his house to be broken up.

Therefore be ye also ready: for in such an hour as ye think not the Son of man cometh.

his passage is a Great Tribulation passage that speaks of the last days, right before the Second Coming of Jesus Christ to the earth. For the Lord's Second Coming is in two stages; the first stage is the Rapture of the Saved (1 Thessalonians 4:13–18) and the second stage is the Millennial Reign of Christ on Earth (Revelation 19–20). God told Noah to warn the people about the coming flood, and they didn't listen, so they were destroyed. They were doing some of everything under the sun (Genesis 6). Before Noah, they had Enoch (Jude) to warn them about the Lord's coming with ten thousands of His saints. As it was in the days of Noah, so it will be at the time of the Lord's coming. People will be doing some of everything under the sun that is ungodly. There is one clear fact: the wicked will be taken as it was in Noah's days (Revelation 19), and the

Lord will use the birds of the air to clean up the dead bodies of the wicked. Please understand that the one taken in the Matthew passage is the wicked; the righteous will be left to enter into the Millennial Kingdom with the Lord (Revelation 20:4–6).

The thing for all saints to keep in mind is that no one knows when the Lord is coming back, so don't allow any preacher, minister, pastor, or believer to tell you when. Jesus Christ is coming back someday, and it will catch people by surprise. All people should get ready and stay ready for the Lord's return. A man does not know when a robber will break into his house; if he did, he would be ready for him just in case he comes. This is why people have security systems in their houses— in case a robber comes. The Holy Spirit is the security for the believer for he knows that the Lord is coming as a thief in the night, and he must be ready. The only way to be ready is to know Jesus Christ and rely on the Holy Spirit to keep and hold you in the Lord. Believers are to live in expectation of the Lord's coming at any moment, but until then, He has His angels coming to take His children home to be with Him.

Are expecting the Lord to come back? What are you doing to warn the lost about the Lord's coming?

Chapter 27
Looking out for the Poor

Leviticus 19:9–15 (KJV)

And when ye reap the harvest of your land, thou shalt not wholly reap the corners of thy field, neither shalt thou gather the gleanings of thy harvest.

And thou shalt not glean thy vineyard, neither shalt thou gather *every* grape of thy vineyard;

thou shalt leave them for the poor and stranger:
I *am* the LORD your God.

Ye shall not steal, neither deal falsely, neither
lie one to another.

And ye shall not swear by my name falsely, neither shalt thou profane the name of thy God: I
am the LORD.

Thou shalt not defraud thy neighbour, neither
rob *him:* the wages of him that is hired shall
not abide with thee all night until the morning.

Thou shalt not curse the deaf, nor put a stum-
blingblock before the blind, but shalt fear thy
God: I *am* the LORD.

Ye shall do no unrighteousness in judgment:
thou shalt not respect the person of the poor,

nor honour the person of the mighty: *but* in righteousness shalt thou judge thy neighbour.

The Lord has always cared the poor, and He wants His people to do the same. When Israel went out to harvest the crops, they were not to gather everything out of the fields. The reason they were not to pick the fields clean was to leave some for the poor. The poor people were not able to purchase land to raise crops for their families. Therefore, the Lord expected Israel to be concerned about the poor and the stranger; after all, God had provided for them. Israel was only to go over their fields once to gather the harvest, and all that was left was for the poor and the stranger. Please take note that Israel was not to gather it for the poor and stranger but just leave it for them. The Lord's plan is for the poor and stranger to not depend on others to do for them what they can do for themselves.

The saints are to have compassion for the poor and the stranger. Showing compassion is not doing everything for a person but helping him to do for himself. The poor and the stranger are to be treated fairly for they are not to be looked down on just because they are in such a condition. Believers are to put themselves in the position of others and treat them as they would want to be treated. The Lord expects saints to look out for those who are down and out (Galatians 6:10) for, in helping them, God is glorified. There are some who are looking for a handout, and believers are to be careful and not enable them by continuing to give them handouts. Instead of giving a handout, give a hand up like the

prophet Elisha gave the widow woman (2 Kings 4:1–7)
by telling her to have her sons to gather empty pots.

Are you available to help the poor and the stranger?
Are you willing to leave something for someone else?
Are you giving handouts or hand ups?

Chapter 28
Remember the Poor

Deuteronomy 15:5–11 (KJV)

If there be among you a poor man of one of
thy brethren within any of thy gates in thy land
which the LORD thy God giveth thee, thou shalt
not harden thine heart, nor shut thine hand from
thy poor brother:

But thou shalt open thine hand wide unto him, and shalt surely lend him sufficient for his need, *in that* which he wanteth.

Beware that there be not a thought in thy wicked heart, saying, The seventh year, the year of release, is at hand; and thine eye be evil against thy poor brother, and thou givest him nought; and he cry unto the LORD against thee, and it be sin unto thee.

Thou shalt surely give him, and thine heart shall not be grieved when thou givest unto him: because that for this thing the LORD thy God shall bless thee in all thy works, and in all that thou puttest thine hand unto.

For the poor shall never cease out of the land: therefore I command thee, saying, Thou shalt

open thine hand wide unto thy brother, to thy
poor, and to thy needy, in thy land.

The Lord wanted Israel to extend an open hand
to give to the poor. When one is blessed by the
Lord, he is to be a blessing to others. Please take note: it
says, "one of thy brethren" this means one in the family
of Israel. God does not want any member of the family
to go without. Every member of the family is to look out
for the others. He is to remember that the Lord gave him
what he has for the purpose of caring for his family and
others who are in need. It is the desire of the Lord for
His people to have a good, ready heart to help when the
need presents itself. John points out in his writing that
it is not right to have the goods and have a closed heart

(1 John 3:17). He wanted to know how one can say he loves the Lord and not care for the needy.

Saints are not to think evil toward the poor and speak badly of them just because they don't have what they need. The Israelites were to free one of any debt on the seventh year, which means whatever he owed was cleared. They were not to attempt to mistreat the poor just because the seventh year was near. If the poor needed something even in the sixth year, they were to help. It was displeasing to the Lord for Israel to turn down a request to help the poor after the Lord had blessed them with everything. It was a sin before the Lord to treat the poor badly. God looks at the motive when believers give to the poor. It is very important when believers give that it is done in the right manner because that is the only way the Lord will accept it (2

Corinthians 9:7). The poor will always be around (John 12:8), so believers will always have something to do.

Why do you help the poor? How do you treat the poor? Do you put down the poor?

Chapter 29
A Party for the Poor

Esther 9:19–23 (KJV)

Therefore the Jews of the villages, that dwelt in the unwalled towns, made the fourteenth day of the month Adar *a day of* gladness and feasting, and a good day, and of sending portions one to another.

And Mordecai wrote these things, and sent letters unto all the Jews that *were* in all the provinces of the king Ahasuerus, *both* nigh and far,

To stablish *this* among them, that they should keep the fourteenth day of the month Adar, and the fifteenth day of the same, yearly,

As the days wherein the Jews rested from their enemies, and the month which was turned unto them from sorrow to joy, and from mourning into a good day: that they should make them days of feasting and joy, and of sending portions one to another, and gifts to the poor.

And the Jews undertook to do as they had begun, and as Mordecai had written unto them;

*I*t was a special day for the Jews who were in domain of King Ahasuerus for it was the fourteenth day of Adar (February or March), a day of

145

gladness. It was a day that they would send gifts to others. Mordecai established this as a special day for the Jews while they were in Persia. They were not in their homeland, and they made the best out of a bad situation. The Lord had given them a victory over their enemies, and it was time to celebrate. Mordecai led them to turn their sorrow into joy, mourning into laughter, and sadness into gladness. In the letter that Mordecai sent out to the Jews, he told them to celebrate two days, the fourteenth and fifteenth of Adar. He wanted his people to have a joyful time that would override all the sadness. One of the greatest things about their gatherings of fellowship, fun, and food was that the poor were not left out. They were concerned about those who did not have the means for a celebration for the poor needed to have a joyful time, also.

There are great lessons from this passage for all believers.

1. Don't allow the enemies to get you down and keep you down.

2. Don't allow your location to keep you from enjoying life.

3. Learn to turn your circumstances around by listening to the leader.

4. Celebrate after a victory.

5. Remember those who don't have the means.

Are you willing to have a dinner and invite the poor? Are you concerned about the poor? Who do you give gifts to? What if you were the only one who didn't have the means to celebrate?

Chapter 30
Remember the Oppressed
Psalm 10:12–18 (KJV)

Arise, O LORD; O God, lift up thine hand:
forget not the humble.

Wherefore doth the wicked contemn God? he
hath said in his heart, Thou wilt not require *it*.

Thou hast seen *it;* for thou beholdest mischief
and spite, to requite *it* with thy hand: the poor

committeth himself unto thee; thou art the helper of the fatherless.

Break thou the arm of the wicked and the evil *man:* seek out his wickedness *till* thou find none.

The LORD *is* King for ever and ever: the heathen are perished out of his land.

LORD, thou hast heard the desire of the humble: thou wilt prepare their heart, thou wilt cause thine ear to hear:

To judge the fatherless and the oppressed, that the man of the earth may no more oppress.

*T*here are times when believers wonder if the Lord cares; it seems as though they are left alone with enemies who are bothering them. This is the case in the first part of this passage. David was

149

praying to God about the things the wicked people were doing. They were making all kinds of attacks on righteous people. He saw how the righteous were hurting because of the wicked. David, like all others, was troubled because it looked like the wicked was getting away with their actions. Therefore, he called on the Lord for help. He wanted God to step in for those who were being oppressed. He says to the Lord, "Don't You see what the righteous is being put through by the enemies?" He desired for the Lord to come right away and stop the enemies.

Saints must always keep in mind that God moves on His own time. He does see and knows what the righteous are going through, and He will step in right on time. God does hear the prayers of the righteous, and He will answer them in time. Believers are to stay humble under the pressures of life and the enemy because God will give them strength. One way saints ought to look at what they are going through is that the Lord is shaping and molding them for the road of life. Therefore, the next time you are being attacked by the enemy, don't give up, don't give in, and don't give out; the Lord is closer than a phone call.

Have you ever felt like giving up? Have you ever thought that you were all alone? Have you ever wondered if God cares? Have you ever called on the Lord? Have you ever been oppressed? Have you ever oppressed anyone?

About the Author

*M*OSES LEE RADFORD was born in Cerulean, Kentucky to the Rev. and Mrs. E. D. Radford on November 19, 1960. He is married to his wife of thirty-four years, Calvonia Louise Vaught

Radford, and they are the parents of Mario Jamil, Casondra Leann, and Christian Leah and god-daughter Toya White. He accepted Christ and was baptized in 1968 at Pleasant Hill Baptist Church of Christian County, Kentucky. He acknowledged the call to preach the Gospel and was ordained as a Baptist minister in 1980 at Pleasant Hill Baptist Church under the pastorate of his father Rev. E. D. Radford.

Rev. Radford was educated through the Trigg County Schools System in Cadiz, Kentucky. He completed seminary work at Andersonville Theological Seminary in Camilla, Georgia, receiving the bachelor degree of Christian education, a master's degree of divinity in pastoral leadership, and a doctor of ministry degree in pastoral leadership.

He has been pastoring for almost thirty-four years, with the last twenty-four and a half years serving First Baptist Church, Nicholasville, Kentucky. He has been very involved in Baptist association works for the past thirty-five years and has served in many capacities. He is a former moderator of Kentucky Missionary Baptist Association.

Rev. Radford is also author of *Jump Start for Preachers and Teachers*. Books that are coming soon are *Jump Start Your Day with the Lord # 2* and *Jump Start for Preachers and Teachers # 2*.

CPSIA information can be obtained
at www.ICGtesting.com
Printed in the USA
LVOW04s0534300816

502359LV00009B/31/P